This Way to the Sugar

ℭℨ

Poems by Hieu Minh Nguyen

WRITEBLOODY
QUALITY AMERICAN BOOKS

Write Bloody Publishing
America's Independent Press

Austin, TX

WRITEBLOODY.COM

This Way to the Sugar

© 2014 Hieu Minh Nguyen

No part of this book may be used or performed without written consent from the author, except for critical articles or reviews.

Hieu Minh Nguyen
First Edition
ISBN: 978-1938912-73-3

Cover art by Ashley Siebels
Cover photo by Ashley Siebels
Proofread by Philip McCaffrey, Dylan Garity, and Neil Hilborn
Edited by Derrick Brown, Sam Sax, Michael Mlekoday, and Danez Smith
Author photo by Michelle Tacheny
Interior layout by Ashley Siebels

Type set in Bergamo from www.theleagueofmoveabletype.com

Write Bloody Publishing
Austin, TX
Support Independent Presses
writebloody.com

To contact the author, send an email to writebloody@gmail.com

THIS WAY TO THE SUGAR

This Way to the Sugar

III

For Stacy, Samantha, and Alexandria

BOY

My mother's favorite story, a dull one, of course—
　　　is that she did not scream during my birth,
instead dug her nails into her sister's wrist, severing
　　　a vein, and killing her—I'm only joking.
She lived. I did say this was her favorite story after all.

:::

They say if the mother is silent
during birth, then the child will grow
up without the ability to smell or decipher
maps, but will indeed grow up.

They say if the baby is born silent,
then it's probably a faggot, or dead,
or will be eventually.

:::

He was a stupid child. Ate dirt they said. Ate glass
and people's wallets. Kept a farm of cigarette butts
in his cheeks. Smelled like a highway,

but sounded like a boy.
Stood on the overpass and swore
he could hear her screaming.

I

"I'm not lost for I know where I am.
But however, where I am may be lost."

— A.A. Milne, Winnie-the-Pooh

A/S/L

Tonight, I am unhooking my jaw.
I am telling him everything

he wants to hear. My breath fogging
up the computer screen like a wet ghost.

I am cracking open my lips with a cherry.
how old r u? I tell him I am 19—I am lying.

I am 14. I tell him my name is Steven—
that's a nice name. I haven't done this

before. He tells me he is 43. *do u mind?*
No. I tell him I am all alone. Painting

myself in leather and candle wax. *Does that turn
you on?* He thinks I smell like sweat

and mint. I am five inches taller, a hundred
pounds lighter. I have green eyes and copper hair.

I've been so naughty. I live next to an orchard
of white lies. I am plucking fuller lips off the vine,

covering my face, my thighs, fat in dirt. I am growing
a bigger dick. I am sending him pictures of strangers.

I don't tell him I am soft. I don't tell him about my history
homework. I tell him, *I am typing with my tongue*

I am so hard. Hanging my clothes out to dry
on a strand of drool. Only responding with *Yes*

and *Yes* and *Yes.* There's no unwilling mouth.
      I am spoon-feeding him

my right arm. I am only here to please, to moisturize
his palms, to spit-shine the screen. *u r perfect*. I am

picturing him faceless, in some dry town,
in a room thick with lights, masturbating

in front of a mirror, to nothing.

McDonough Homes

The only thing that separated my house
from the mother of six who drowned
each one of her kids in the bathtub
was the neighborhood playground.
The entire street sat on their stoops
and watched the six body bags leak
from underneath that door.

When the woman at the end
of my block tossed her newborn twins
off the Wabasha Street Bridge
on the 4th of July like confetti
from a cannon, all of the children
started locking their bedroom doors.
Scared of toxic food and a sickness
that we all assumed contagious.
Every time my mother drew a bath,
I assumed it was for me.

WHEN THE NEIGHBOR BOYS GATHERED

It seemed all their faces grew
sticky as they watched. Fruit flies stuck to their chins.

Like any soft boy, I am constantly reminded
of how much better I look

inside-out. It was in Kevin's backyard
where I learned how to swallow

a boot or two.
This was the birthplace of my knees,

new cells coating the gravel, red lesions
like fat worms along my legs.

I didn't always hate them—the boys I mean.
It was the closest I've come to baptism.

Head locked against his naked torso. His sour sweat
burning my eyes shut. That restless timbre

growing in my head, as I pursed my lips and pressed
my face into his ribs, left a trail of saliva

along his bare skin. Muscles withered
and dried out as he pushed me away, disgusted

at how hard my pulse had become
in his arms. This is how the summer opened

its wet mouth, how it wrung the blood
from a body and rebuilt it
from the mud.

Buffet Etiquette

My mother and I don't have dinner table conversations
out of courtesy. We don't want to remind each other
of our accents. Her voice, a Vietnamese lullaby
sung to an empty bed. The taste of her hometown
still kicking on the back of her teeth.

My voice is bleach. My voice has no history.
My voice is the ringing of an empty picture frame.

:::

I am forgetting how to say the simple things
to my mother. The words that linger in my periphery.
The words, a rear view mirror dangling from the wires.
I am only fluent in apologies.

:::

Sometimes when I watch home movies, I don't even understand
myself. My childhood is a foreign film. All of my memories
have been dubbed in English.

:::

My mother's favorite television shows are all 90s sitcoms.
The ones that have laugh tracks. The prerecorded emotion
that cues her when to smile.

:::

In the first grade, I mastered my tongue. I cleaned
my speech, and during parent-teacher conferences
Mrs. Turner was surprised my mother was Asian.
She just assumed I was adopted. She assumed
that this voice was the same one I started with.

:::

As she holds a pair of chopsticks, a friend asks me
why I am using a fork. I tell her it's much easier.
With her voice the same octave as my grandmother's,
she says, "but this is so much cooler."

:::

I am just the clip-art. The poster boy of whitewash. My skin
has been burning easier these days. My voice box is shrinking.
I have rinsed it out too many times.

:::

My house is a silent film.
My house is infested with subtitles.

:::

That's all.   That's all.
I have nothing else to say

TATER TOT HOTDISH

The year my family discovered finger food
recipes, they replaced the roast duck with a turkey,
the rice became a platter of cheese and crackers,
none of us complained. We all hated the way the fish
sauce made our breath smell. When the women
started lightening their hair, we blamed it on the sun.
When Emily showed up with blonde highlights
and an ivory boyfriend, we all started talking
about mixed babies—overjoyed with the possibility
of blue eyes in the family photo. That year
I started misspelling my last name, started reshaping
myself to have a more phonetic face. Vietnam
became a place our family pitied, a thirsty rat
with hair too dark and a scowl too thick.
We stopped going to temple and found ourselves
a church. That year my mother closed her eyes
and bowed her head to prayers she couldn't understand.

HIEU HUEY

if you choose to drown   leave the amputated limb
in a sea crawling with tradition,   begging to be more useful
relax that heavy head   and someone else will find it
sinking in a mud pit   stuffed with grenade pins,
and when you wake up,   the remains of your mother's home
holding your sore mouth,   responsible for false devotion.
start praying that   your body will soon reject
the mothers desperate for   the bullet shells in your back and their
values won't turn away that hungry   swarm of arrowheads aimed at the sun's
face, giving you the empty side of the   horizon, asking to be left decorating the
dinner table, a cautious compromise,   new bodies, splayed, and welcoming
the half-open hands   the native land and our new home.

It Was the Winter We Learned How To Properly Smoke a Cigarette, or It Was the Spring We Finally Found Brooke Parker's Dog, Mango, After All the Snow Had Melted

After Daniel's funeral, we made a papier-mâché piñata
        from leftover programs, filled it

with dandelion seeds and tried to beat the wishes out of them. I think
        we were nine. I could be lying. But I distinctly remember

you losing your last three baby teeth after your dad bounced your face
        off of the garage door. Maybe it was

just a very vivid dream. Nostalgia forgets to visit this street.
        It is too busy with tree houses and rope swings.

It doesn't have time for all of this gray. All of my favorite memories
        have been the ones away from home. It might have been

the summer I broke my wrist, or maybe it was the summer
        your mom started selling little bags

out of your basement, or maybe it was the summer of both,
        when we stuffed our backpacks with cereal

and ran away to a playground three miles from home—
        I think we biked, or walked, or maybe it was the summer

you stole your parents' bright green Buick. We arrived at that sandbox
        and ran to the swing set out of habit.

There was no rust there. I didn't believe I was swinging
        cause I couldn't hear that scrape above

my head, I couldn't feel the buzz of a saw blade. That land,
        a white gown, shapeless and unflattering

in our dingy light. In that foreign America they must consider
    the dandelion a weed—not a bouquet

of potential. I remember listening to the other children's voices
    as their porch lights beckoned them home

for supper, ditching their mosquito halos by the tire swing.
    How they sounded like children.

How they walked, and jumped, and sang like children.

FLIGHT

after Sam Sax

At the bottom of Heaven's sliding glass door:
a row of gay boys.   Each mistaking death for flight,
                and here: the river
                        looks most like the sky.
And there: a cadaver is siphoned
          through the faucet.   In a dream: my love
buries me alive. I've heard if you die in a dream,
                you die in real life—it's not true. I've tested
the lucid edges of nothing,   and still wake up.
Still here. Sometimes
          you don't die when you're supposed to,
                        and sometimes you do.
Sometimes the gun doesn't fall
                neatly to your side after
                        the trigger is pulled,
and you are found in the bathtub
                with the barrel still hot
                        in your mouth.
                How embarrassing.   Caught bursting
                                at the cowlick.
It's not what you'd expect,   not like the movies at all.
                                You lose teeth.

GIRLS

The story begins differently in my head—
one version which sounds a lot like laughter
rolling its wet body into the fire and killing
the lights, but my version is more
like four boys standing at the edge of a lake,
unbuttoning their shirts while panties float
to shore. Undressing the timid night,
trying to make out those giggling shapes
we see shifting in the distance, beckoning us
to lay our bodies on the moon's white tongue,
to feel the water fill the spaces that have gone
untouched. Before the night is done,
before each eager boy is waist-deep
in a song that doesn't fit in my mouth,
the tide pushed my saltless body back to shore.
Taunting me with a song
that drifted farther and farther away.

THE HAND THAT FED

When I was nine, the dog with no name
bloomed a civilization of hives across my body.
His saliva left me collecting ribbons of skin
underneath my nails, but I loved him
the way I love the relief of scratching.

One day I came home from school
to learn he gained a new home
and a name—I think it was Brownie—
it doesn't matter. He had a name,
and was no longer mine.

The year I fell into that girl's ocean
like a lost boat, the year guided
by a burning building instead
of a lighthouse, I started waking
from the thickest hour of sleep to a howling
mutt outside my window, so sure
that he had returned for me. That vengeful
abandoned dander threatening to gnaw
and bubble my flesh, my laughable armor.

When I put a name to it, told her that I loved
her, I could feel my throat beginning to blister.

ARRANGEMENT

my grandmother tells me you are very pretty
your smile not of a girl but of a package
teeth straight and perfectly arranged
like each petal in a bride's bouquet

your smile not of a girl but of a package
you are presented to me as a trophy
like each petal in a bride's bouquet
a haunting hiding underneath a veil

you are presented to me as a trophy
in my sheets there's a continent between us
a haunting hiding underneath a veil
we will sleep in separate beds

in my sheets there's a continent between us
wedding photos hang in the walk-in closet
we will sleep in separate beds
make a habit out of undressing in the bathroom

wedding photos hang in the walk-in closet
teeth straight and perfectly arranged
make a habit out of undressing in the bathroom
my grandmother tells me you are very pretty

My First

The car is filling with water so I plug the hole with a pudgy finger.
        This always happens to me, which is to say: the ocean
                is always happening.
There is a man unzipping his pants
        in the passenger seat and a school of shiny fish
in the rear-view, like a sequin gown
                brought to life by salt.
I don't know his name. He could be my father,
        but is not my father
           since he is white, and here,
                and easily impressed
    by the way I roll my neck.
        This is not a dream. Don't pinch me.
      I won't tell you how I survived the wreckage.
This story doesn't leave the ocean floor.
          This story went away, bleached
    clean. In an earlier version
        that man became a girl,
          and then, years later, a creature.
      Tentacles dripping with grease, glowing
            white eyes.
Am I lying again? The opposite
           of helpful is not helpful,
    which a life raft would be. I don't need to be saved.
The opposite of touch is bleeding. The ocean swallows
      all the colors, and will never stop
trying to get inside my body.   In the current
        draft I tell: he becomes a man again,
    and then a man shriveled
      when met with salt.

Teacher's Pet

I ride the bus the entire way
with the cold peaches sweating

in my upturned shirt. The fruit rolls
across the table and onto her office floor.

An apple, though a tougher breed,
would have been too cliché. I hand her the one

I believe to be the sweetest, the one opened
by the carpet's rough skin. Peeling the sugared

meat from the ground like separating a wound
from a gauze bandage, I raise the borderless fruit

to her mouth, holding it above my head, a gift
already unwrapped. She buries her face into my

small palms and slurps the juice, the syrup
dripping into my hair. Her clean fist wipes

the gloss from her chin and a small boy
stuck to the back of her hand.

HALLOWEEN, 14

Of course it was a bad idea
sending my address
to that headless gentleman—
jack-o-lantern's smile, out of frame,
assumed he would come on a dark horse,
not unlike a prince. I invited him over
while mother slept in the next room,
exhausted from hiding in our dark house
when the neighbor kids, who tonight,
covered themselves in blood
and pretended it was a costume, drummed
with laughter while they pissed
on our lightless porch—round here
we don't pass out candy, round here
you ask your neighbor for a cup of sugar
and she hands you her newborn—
don't you dare give it back. Don't
you dare try to coddle it into silence.
You let it cry and cry until it grows
up and urinates on your mother's
basil, until the whole goddamn street
glows and smells of burning bags
of shit, or at least that's the smell
I remember when I think of that night,
think of darkness being watered
thin, think of that man, who sat
in his humming car for three hours
chain-smoking, headlights pointed
towards my bedroom window, calling
and calling, whispering some name I forgot
I'd given him, waiting for a bloodless boy
to come out from hiding.

II

"Would it be possible to find a more ungrateful boy,
or one with less heart than I have?"

— Carlo Collodi, Pinocchio

THE OCEAN, MAYBE

He didn't expect me to be that fat,
didn't anticipate the extra weight

he had to carry. But since I am
already here and warm enough

to cradle a pulse in a wilting man,
since the moon is waning (or waxing,

never could tell, really) on the other side
of the city, since the dogs snarling and barking

in the doorway have stopped and grown
accustomed to my scent, since the buses

will stop running soon, and the other men,
by now, will be too drunk to drive, or hold

an erection, since I've made an attempt
to look at least halfway decent, to be more

than pixels, since my body is a sea,
a good sea, the ocean, maybe,

since I've trained my mouth to suck
the bullets out of dead men,

I don't have to learn his name,
since I am, after all, a grain of glass

on a waterline, cutting open
his eyes every time he blinks.

Teacher's Pet

Know: I am somewhat grateful for this body, this ugly,
this slow metabolism, and these layers and layers.

                                        I am not saying

I'd be beautiful thinner—I tried that already, got plenty of affection
from that woman with the smudged face and melting fingers,

                                those claw marks

that rise to the surface of all these stretched cells. I have built myself
a safer body, covered the rot with rot. Sometimes I can hear that little
      boy

                                I tucked away,

lost in this new house, gasping for breath, or another meal, or her,
the woman that held our name in her mouth like a Eucharist wafer,

                                or a wet god,

and maybe praying was enough, maybe the scars weren't necessary
to ward off spirits from this secondhand husk. Something wicked

                                has occupied me

for years, wallpaper dressed in bitter smoke, a chandelier
of unbrushed teeth, a school of birds picked and pecked,

                                upturned the lawn,

until I woke up holding a pair of scissors and a fist
clenching the parts of me that had already died,

                                there's no need

to eradicate this vessel of shadows. Lightning
won't strike twice on a vandalized house.

It Was the Morning He Discovered Chicken Bones Under My Pillow, or It Was the Night I Drank, and Drank, and Drank Until I Finally Found My Keys At the Bottom of Lake Harriet

Bellyache humming a dull
sailor's tune. Boy with sugar

in his tank. The organ,
the origin, life-sized and growing

legs, growing fever and a dry
sense of humor. Laughing

and clutching a gut, a headboard,
another boy's genitals. Another god

to blame for a sleepless night.
A body filling with ghost stories,

gutted by mood lighting. A house
filling with a magician's dirty laundry.

What privilege to smell sulfur
and assume candles?

The heat was supposed to break
a month ago—wait for it ..nope.

Still hot, still thick and graceless,
smoke still in midair. Still here.

Two weeks facedown in the mud.
Drunk—at least I think we are.

Lovesick—I'm sure we're not
the only ones starving. Some myth,

right? Some god, right? Take this body
and see a body, where so many see a grave.

Come! See: the ugliest mouth
on both sides of the Mississippi.

CHOKE

Perhaps my body would make more sense
if you cut it open. A door that swings
at the throat. Your lap stripping

the wet carpet of my mouth, prying loose
the marble tiles. Tell me if you know
an affordable magician with hands

steady enough to sever a torso and conjure,
from this heaving carcass, the rabbit's bones.
If I say: *your father taught me how to smile*

a real man's width, I would be lying, though
I'm almost certain he had a child. There is a boy
wailing in the distance, but that too could be me,

or my hunger, which rises with every person
it swallows. My cheeks swell
with sand, and I close my mouth,

and there's no other exit, no way out,
just some man spreading his light
at the end of the tunnel.

TEACHER'S PET

When you remember her face
for the first time in ten years,
you are across the aisle from a man
who looks nothing like her,
but somehow you recall the night
she came to your house
and how she flinched
when your mother thanked her
for dropping off your backpack.
Think back to the way you felt
when she called other children
to her office, how relief was a house
painted green. Remember the way
she recoiled when you called her
mommy, or how she kissed
your forehead before you boarded
the bus, on your way back home.

DRY

When I warned my mother
about the mold starting to grow
along the bathroom tiles,
she simply put a rug over it.
She ignored it for months.

Engulfed by a storm
cloud, the pink shag began
to transform. Soon lost in the skin
of a wild animal, the tiles became
the gray scales of a dragon,
but my mother kept on ignoring

the smoke, the bullet holes
in the toilet tank, the masked man
behind the shower curtain.

Have you heard of the boys
who turn wolf in moonlight?
Or the women who turn mother
at the foot of a hospital bed?

Such careless children
to let the piercing get infected
to the point of amputation.
To cover the scab with a fucking rug.

When the men came in white
to gut our porcelain wound, she blamed me
for it all, the leather-coated ceramic, the bill,
the spores reupholstering my lungs with wool.

NOURISH

I see the boy gleaming underneath the neighbor's
        motion detectors, face cut
with the clothesline's shadow, like his mouth
        is frothing with tar,
or blueberries, or maybe that's what hunger looks like,
        like a forty-minute drive,
like gas money, and I want to ask him how much he spent
        to get here, so I can offer half, or at least
know how much I am worth, so later, when he's pulling out
        my spine with whatever instrument
makes the least amount of noise, I can gauge the right amount
        of soap and boil, or maybe just lay
in its filth, like that dinner table with the plates rusting over,
        how I promised to clear it last week,
but just fell asleep on the couch with my pants unbuttoned.

THE DOCK

No one wants to go near the lake
that swallowed two more boys

this year. Sad story, yes, but we're thankful
to have a pretty place to be discreet.

Not saying a basement can't be pretty,
and don't get me wrong, I am a fan

of the mass-produced hotel art,
the same photo hanging above each bed

makes it easier to pretend each new room
is still our room, makes me crave a life

of dull decor and basic cable, makes my mouth
water, really. I bite the lips off of a Styrofoam cup

and spit them at the ducks that swim past.
Wait. Don't eat that. Fuck.

This is the first time I hear him laugh out loud.
With him, there are few noises I can recognize.

A fly lands on his cheek and I try to brush it
away, but before my hand can cast

a shadow on the bridge of his nose,
the fly burrows into him. He doesn't flinch,

just winks—and now there's one on his knee,
and another lands in his dimple, one on each

eyelid. There are hundreds now, all digging
or moving underneath his skin, all bubbling

behind that firm smile. His eyes begin
to vibrate, and he doesn't reach for me. He doesn't

need me here, really. I am no expert, or exorcist,
or great love. I am just another boy sitting

an arm's length away from someone he doesn't recognize
in the light. He opens his mouth and they all fly out,

not a swarm, but a single-file line, a thin braid of black
hair, the longest exhale from a sinking car—that's it.

There. That's the noise I'm so familiar with.

DEAR FRIEND

for JD

It's another winter
I've refuse to wear mittens,
and still my hands are here—
tell me again of the cold
that far north of daylight,
or sing me a song
I will never make the effort
to understand.
Do you tell the story of us?
The boy you found digging
a hole in a whale's back,
or is it the clean version
where you drive across the country
just to be disappointed
by the ocean, or you drive
across the country just to think
about calling? If the tale starts
in winter, then you are already gone.
I tell you I am happy,
and you tell me you are happy,
and I am told I'm supposed to
hate you, since hate is the body
that stays when love leaves,
but by now that skin has a new name,
and if the story of us begins
in summer, then I'm the one who left.
I'm the one who buried everything
that had a face.

THE GAY 90S,
MINNEAPOLIS, MINNESOTA, 18+

after Sierra DeMulder

This is where the straight people go
to watch *The Gays*. They come
wearing pride and proud in fishnet
costumes. They come to watch the main event
of smoke and sweat and mirrors.

We are your #1 fans! They have all come
to The Show: See the Cock Swallower.
The Dancing Bears. Come watch those Strong
Women. The Married Men
all cramming into one bathroom stall.

Bring a beard and a moist towelette.
It's a five-dollar cover. It's a good time. Tip
the bartender,

smile for the cameras, twirl for the fire.
The audience is watching. They are waiting
for you to do a trick.

AT THE SUPERMARKET

I find my mother's shopping cart in the middle of the aisle with her nowhere in sight, purse still in the cart, eggs crushed underneath soup cans. She is not in this aisle or the next or the one with the deodorant. When I hear a pyramid of jars collapse, I look for her clumsy hands. I am disappointed to find a small child standing in a pool of green juice. *Ugh. Where are your parents, kid?* A scream from the checkout lane, a stampede of grapefruits, all belonging to someone else. My voice, a hot stone curdling the dairy, the creamer, that lady's breast. A kind stranger helps me call for her. He doesn't know he is saying the Vietnamese word for mother. He assumes that he is saying a child's name. This makes her more important. This makes her hunger a room filling with sand, her world darker, slicked with ice and sharp edges. The bathrooms are a hopeless and empty playground. The parking lot, a scatter of mothers with bumper sticker faces. The children, packed meat, all squeaking their cellophane song. This way to the sugar. This way to the dairy. Aisle four aisle five six seven bakery meat deli. And of course just like that, just like traffic, or magic, or winter, she is there, cradling a watermelon like a ball that rolled and just kept on rolling, until it stopped at the lips of a cave or a strange man or a semi truck. She drops the watermelon into the cart, on top of the tomatoes.

CHRISTMAS EVE, 17

The only goodnight kiss I would
receive came from the bright burst

of headlights as he backed out
of the hotel parking lot. Each raw

knee, puffy with the negative imprints
of the carpet's braided teeth. Only the sink

has hot water. No point in showering
when sweat is no longer sweat. You can

no longer see his pulse's splatter across
the palette. The paint is a different color

when it dries. It's like he was never here.
The gift was rewrapped. A garland

of meat, unstrung. The glass is full.
Again. Again. The mouth, a clean

gutter. The body, a buffed wall.
This never happened. The botched

deconstruction, tooth by tooth,
each growing back. Smile

digging its way out of a pink grave.
Everything is fine. Nothing is gone.

DIFFUSE

Their arms reaching over   me, like a bridge,
        or a tightrope over some electric pool. Finger-diving
into each other's backs.   I am still
                fully dressed, and maybe I'm a prude,
                        or maybe I thought
some eager mouth would find me.
                        I guess
that's what I get for thinking of myself half-full,
        or even water at all, or even cold. Y'know
you're not supposed to
        be cold. Not with this many people
in a bed. When they finally notice me
                        kissing their shoulders,
        like a dog eating
off the dinner table, they both kiss me.
        A thousand swelling hairs on my tongue.
                        They taste the same,
and I know I'm probably watering
                down the flavor,
        I'm probably diffusing the boil, and the boy
that brought me here says he wants to expose me
                to great things. He opens my throat,
                        a disposable gutter, and I know
                        I'm empty
or full, or which one he wants me to be, but I hope
        it's the right one, and I don't know who's holding my face
to the mattress, the one that wanted to salt my spine,
                or the one that wanted to tag along
                        and sing some wicked lullaby,
but I hope it's the right one.
It's a miracle that I haven't spilled over, really is
        some kind of blessing that this accordion torso
                has yet to break open with its hideous yawn,
and I should consider myself lucky   enough to feel
                a current pass through me
even if it settles in someone else. There is honor in being a message

in a bottle, or just the bottle,

empty,

full, jagged. Don't kiss the messenger, don't fuck
the middleman,   or do, and watch the sweat
bead, and then disappear.

LADYBOY THEATER

It's not that I wanted to fuck him cause he was white,
or that I pitied him for wanting me in that moment,
a desperate man drinking his own urine to survive.
This is no desert—the West, maybe, but he called me
easy, and all I could do to prove him wrong was swallow.

:::

[sunrise]

Boy in a dress does a fan dance
with a severed hand. Cherry blossoms
dripping from his small cock.
Bow for the savior. Kneel for your god.
Fall on his sword.

:::

Mistermister, did you know my father
snuck over to Cambodia from Vietnam?
He capsized his own boat
before he made it to shore
so the guards would rescue him
instead of shooting.

Don't you know brown boys
are always drowning?
You can put that gun down.

:::

[dusk]

Boy undressed, jabs a hair ornament
into the hero's neck as he cums.
I heard Batman was a rice queen on the low.
Chopstick eroticism: maneuver your thumbs,
crack me in half.

:::

Mistermister, do you expect a happy ending?
You told me I was beautiful as if it was something
I wouldn't hear without you.

:::

[dawn]

Boy in a dress performs a tea ceremony
on all fours. Bent in like a river.
Incense burning down, ash crumbling
into the small of his back. Human sushi
platter. Human spice rack. Human-sized mouth.

:::

Mistermister, do you hear that train coming?
My kin made this bed of spikes.
My kin made theses silk chains. Probably
that ball gag too. There's no time, sir.
Save yourself. Just put that penny
on my forehead and step out of the way.

:::

boy   lathers in a tub of saké.
boy   fresh off the poppers.
boy   mail ordered.
boy   the wrong package.
boy   dog collar made from jade.
boy   rice wine enema.
boy   napalm bukakke.

:::

[sunset]

Boy in a dress waits in a burning temple for a soldier
to come save him. White man runs down an endless hill
trampling over the faces of a nation of mothers.
The bullets come. The bullets hit. Their daughters
gone. Their daughters mall-walking with a white child
on a leash.

TEACHER'S PET

How do I describe what happened to me
if I'm not entirely sure what happened
to me? Therapy brings no closure,
instead, an echo that loses her name deeper
inside my body. I am a well of faceless
coins. I've tried to dig her out
of the marble, but have only managed to sculpt
a pair of hands. These are her hands.
I am starting to remember them quite
well. I remember digesting them inside her
office as she loosened the wet denim suctioned
to my nine-year-old thigh, peeling away everything
gold-soaked and warm. I am on her lap
now, my face being pressed against her
freckled chest. The musky smell of tangy
leather has yet to fade from the bridge
of my nose. Sometimes I can smell her
on a crowded bus or still stitched to the collar
of a secondhand blouse. If I close my eyes,
I am there. Here. Inches away from the wafting
scent of citrus and decay. I can almost make out
her face. Her voice peels away the top layer
of keratin from my nails. Warmth leaves
my body. Gold runs down a leg.

III

"When ladies used to come to me in dreams,
I said, 'Pretty mother, pretty mother.'
But when at last she really came, I shot her."

— J.M. Barrie, Peter Pan

Easter, 8

It's almost like the window shattered
on its own, since we never could
prove what hit the back of Carol's head,
and we swore we found nothing
amongst the broken glass, no ransom note
taped to a brick, no bullet still smoking
in the wall, all the children lined up
to be scolded by our mothers, and Vivian,
not my mother, but the white neighbor
lady that brought me along to a suburban house
with a pond in the backyard, where her sister,
in a porcelain gown, pats Vivian's back
and says, *you're doing such a good thing,*
and points her smile, thin as bat wings,
in my direction, and V:v, not my mother,
but told, *he's so well-behaved, you should
adopt him,* ruffles my black hair,
while the other children cry, their glass cracking
cries, after being banned from playing outside,
and I sit, like a good pet, on the couch, and smile
my good smile, *keep him, you should keep him,*
and she feeds me a thick slice of ham, teeth coated
in honey, when I ask if I could help clean
the dishes, help earn my keep, and simultaneously
all their heads roll back, and they laugh a clean laugh,
cause I am a guest, and will always remain just a guest,
and later when this beast is returned
to the wild, my mother will carry
my sleeping body from the car and pull,
from my pocket, a handful of rocks.

TEACHER'S PET

There is a finger   starting to unlace that winter
                            I assumed was just snow.
       The name and face still   thawing, most of this story
yet to come up for air.   Only her hands.
                             It took me
thirteen years to remember those   lingering
    starched digits   on my hip.   How easy it was
                                 to bury them
           underneath nostalgia,   to remember
that age
    only as a swarm of missing   teeth and tokens—
           I could be a liar.   I could be remembering
the wrong details.   Details.   Details: her office is still
    a lost thing.   Darkness holding the ember hostage.
There is nothing in this story that's not a dagger.
                       Her voice is mud
                         sticky
and her name is trying to push its way through
            my gums.
My thighs glow like a fresh scar.   Gravel dripping
            like sweat from my stretched pores.
    All of this
    could just be my sleep   talking. I have come
across many   with her calloused tentacles: cashiers,
      librarians, friends,   men, fingers trained
        in zipper etiquette
and have asked them all to help me   pull back this heavy scab—
                     I'm sorry.
        I've seen your hands
        before. I don't know when,
        but I'm certain they were here.

I Want Nothing

to do with my mother's
sadness, her mouth:
a pockmark on every door
that opens onto a memorial scene,
her mouth: the beginning
of traffic. Odd to think
of it as an ugly and frequent
song on the radio,
a small bird shitting
and dying in my hands.
He is dead, she says,
over and over again,
except in Vietnamese,
which to me doesn't sound
as tragic—a little uglier,
maybe, but less tragic,
for sure. The house phone
on her lap sings its dead
hum into the static air
of our living room. *Who?*
Who? I ask. I shake her
shoulders, *Who?*
When she finally looks
at me through the slit
of her black bangs,
she tells me about the man
she would have married
if she stayed in Vietnam,
and my posture straightens,
and my eyes roll, and I am
relieved at the absence
of my own grief, and I hate him,
this man, this dead man
that won't stay gone
now that he's gone
for good, now that he has built

this house of meat to rot
and stew on the sunniest days,
now that he fills the marrow
in each bone of my mother's
regret. When she thinks of love
either she's a widow or divorced,
and I believed for a while
that regret is leaving
the burning house
empty-handed, but he is
already ash, and I tell her
she made the right choice,
which is funny, cause I hate
my father, and often forget
that he's still alive.

STUBBORN INERITANCE

After we put my grandmother to sleep
in an incinerator, they returned her

to us in a tin cube along with a plastic bag
full of things that refused to melt: nails, screws,

a titanium kneecap. Her wedding ring,
still solid, was placed in the urn surrounded by her

dust, her, and I thought skin was the only thing
holding one's body together. She sat on the bookshelf

for months. Not sure what to do with our beloved
debris. What mountain or gust of wind? What seaside

cliff or bathroom drain? Whose lungs would take her
on a grand adventure? Most of her jingling joints kept

in a Ziploc bag, like bullets, serving no purpose
outside of a body—It took my mother eight years

to accept me for being gay. For eight years I sat
and watched my house burn. I watched her save the baby

photos but leave the baby—I know I should be grateful
that she came around at all. That she forgave me.

I've been told that it's not her fault. It is how she was
raised. I've been told it's our family's old way

of thinking. I've been told to forgive this
stubborn inheritance, this thing that has lived

inside her, and her mother, and her mother's father—
I've been told that once you've been stabbed, it is better to leave

the blade inside the body—removing the dagger will only open
the wound further. Forgiveness will bleed you thin. If you ignore

it, your skin could close around the metal. This is a part of you
now, this is all you will find when my body crumbles, this vengeful

child, this shiny grudge, a thirteen-year-old boy crawling
from the ashes, holding a gas can in his hands.

THE STORY

My mother opens my bedroom
door and gags on the overwhelming scent

of urine, *like something died*, she says,
in the story that follows me

to every family gathering,
a hound locked on the scent

of a wandering child. It was a phase
my mother said lasted until I was fourteen,

or around the time I started doing my own laundry.
She goes on to tell them about the piles of wet

clothes hidden in the back of my closet,
like something died—again

we all know this story,
a boy gets touched and then ruins

the upholstery, or a boy rubs himself
in the back of the school bus

until his jeans become a shade darker.
I never told my mother I was molested,

never told her that story, the one
where a boy finds a tongue,

ten years later, fermenting
in a jar. I never told her

how someone reached inside me
and turned on all the faucets.

In the End

I am told I have to climb
the Mountain of Forgiveness
but I've heard at the top
there is nothing
but a shitty view.

Finally, the Son Talks About Women

after Rachel McKibbens

For the past fifteen years I have chased away all of my mother's suitors. Many have come bearing bouquets of promise and left with a scar the size of my smile. Many flinch when I laugh. Behind the lips I have inherited from my mother are the snarling teeth of my father. No one ever taught me how to be in love with a man. I have gnawed through the joints of every boy that has slept in my bed. Mouth full of gristle.

I am the last man standing in my family. The rest have left guided either by death or free will. I am the only son in a family of daughters and mothers and fire-breathers and lumber-women who crafted their homes from bear traps and chicken broth. These women have trained me to light a matchstick with a tongue, to hold a hand without the need to squeeze, to comb away my cowlicks that sprout my father's matted fur, that canine widow's peak that won't stop growing. These women have soldered a seal of trust with the iron in my blood. My mother tells me I am worthy of a woman's love. This is a compliment. This is the faith that comes before you take the muzzle off, when you turn your back toward a dark alley, when you unhook the leash and expect him to stay.

VISTING HOURS

By now I should know my way around
Regions Hospital. It is the hospital I was born
in, the one that took my tonsils and my grandmother,
gave me three cousins and many, many blood
results. The smell of cold linen and piss
hovers in the thin air of the central tower,
a sour perfume. Her room illuminated
by the monitors, and a late night infomercial on mute—
think it was a blender—behind the curtain divider
she shared the room with a pair of wrists that tried conjuring
some red sea-witch to form in its palms, but if we think about it
this way then she is only a heart that locked its doors and left
the water running, or maybe she is a throat
that couldn't contain its howl, or maybe a fist, or ankle,
or heart, or teeth, or heart, by now she must be a whole body.
By now she must have a name, a whole face, maybe,
and I did not come here to make her laugh,
or fluff her pillows, or spoon-feed her sugar,
to chew-n-spit concern into her dry mouth, but I do.
I brush her hair and wipe the applesauce from her chin,
and she doesn't remember why she's here,
just that she's here. She's home, and her shoes are off
and her sheets are clean, and she prefers it here.
When she is finally discharged, she tells me
that she doesn't want to leave. She tells me she's afraid
of being alone. Such a cliché fear, like heights,
or death, or becoming your mother.

NOSTOPHOBIA

fear of returning home

I am not afraid of the sadness
I will feel when my mother passes—
the undeniable pickaxe of loss
that will lodge itself in front
of me, cutting in line and standing
there forever like proud traffic,
a reminder that I do actually love
her. I am not afraid of the grief
that will haunt burnt eggs, or the crunch
of undercooked rice. Grief like sugar
boiling on a tongue. I am terrified
of no longer being a son,
to have to attend a funeral
without her.

ACKNOWLEDGMENTS

I would like to thank the following journals in which versions of these poems, sometimes under different titles, first appeared:

Anti-: "It Was the Morning He Discovered Chicken Bones Under My Pillow, or It Was the Night I Drank, and Drank, and Drank Until I Finally Found My Keys at the Bottom of Lake Harriet"

The Bakery: "Teacher's Pet [Know: I am]"; "Teacher's Pet [How do I]"

decomP magazinE: "Buffet Etiquette"

Indiana Review: "The Dock"; "The Ocean, Maybe"

The Journal: "A/S/L"; "Diffuse"

Muzzle Magazine: "Nourish"

PANK: "Christmas Eve, 17"

Radius: "Arranged"; "The Gay 90's, Minneapolis, Mn, 18+"; "Tater Tot Hotdish"

Word Riot: "The Hand that Fed"

For their guidance, friendship, support, and wisdom—I wish to thank:

Samuel Sax, Michael Mlekoday, Sierra DeMulder, Danez Smith, Neil Hilborn, Franny Choi, Aaron Samuels, Cam Awkward-Rich, Fatimah Asghar, Rachel Rostad, Ed Bok Lee, Bao Phi, Samuel Cook, Michael Lee, Allison Broeren, Amanda Dakenburgen, Steph-Anne Hobonski, Steven Rentevans, Kate Rokostone, Tish Jones, Cynthia French, Pauline Johnson, Aziza Barnes, Khary Jackson, Kyle Tran Myhre, Ashley Foucault, William Walraven, Samuel James, Jan Mandell, Kat Jordahl, Clara Hutchinson, Matthew Shipman, Jérôme Duchaine, Sarah Rock, Dylan Garity, Samantha Minneart, Alex Minneart, Stacy Nguyen, Amy Nguyen, Emily Nguyen, Kimberly Lynn, The Hubertys.

To Central Touring Theatre, Word Sprout, the Clavicle Collective, and Button Poetry—for always saving me a seat.

To Derrick Brown, and the whole Write Bloody family—for the opportunity, and encouragement.

And lastly, thank you to my mother, Thuan Nguyen, and my grandmother, Bay Thi Tran; the only house I know.

I am the luckiest.

About the Author

Hieu Minh Nguyen was born and raised in Saint Paul, Minnesota, by a single, Vietnamese-American, mother. His work has also appeared in publications such as The Journal, PANK, Anti-, Muzzle, Indiana Review, and other journals. He is a curator for "Inside Voices" a reading series presented by Button Poetry, an organization dedicated to publishing, producing, and promoting poetry.

If You Like Hieu Minh Nguyen, Hieu Minh Nguyen Likes. . .

Floating, Brilliant, Gone
Franny Choi

New Shoes on a Dead Horse
Sierra DeMulder

Racing Hummingbirds
Jeanann Verlee

Good Grief
Stevie Edwards

Reasons to Leave the Slaughter
Benjamin Clark

The New Clean
Jon Sands

Yarmulkes and Fitted Caps
Aaron Samuels

Write Bloody Publishing distributes and promotes great books of fiction, poetry, and art every year. We are an independent press dedicated to quality literature and book design, with an office in Austin, TX.

Our employees are authors and artists, so we call ourselves a family. Our design team comes from all over America: modern painters, photographers, and rock album designers create book covers we're proud to be judged by.

We publish and promote 8 to 12 tour-savvy authors per year. We are grass-roots, D.I.Y., bootstrap believers. Pull up a good book and join the family. Support independent authors, artists, and presses.

**Want to know more about Write Bloody books, authors, and events?
Join our mailing list at**

www.writebloody.com

WRITEBLOODY
QUALITY AMERICAN BOOKS

WRITE BLOODY BOOKS

www.ingramcontent.com/pod-product-compliance
Lightning Source LLC
Chambersburg PA
CBHW030500100426
42813CB00002B/292